"This generation of Christians inhabit cultures that sometimes reject not only biblical revelation about reality, but also the reality of reality itself. The Questions for Restless Minds series poses many of the toughest questions faced by young Christians to some of the world's foremost Christian thinkers and leaders. Along the way, this series seeks to help the Christian next generation to learn how to think biblically when they face questions in years to come that perhaps no one yet sees coming."

—Russell Moore,
public theologian, *Christianity Today*

"If you're hungry to go deeper in your faith, wrestle with hard questions, and are dissatisfied with the shallow content on your social media newsfeed, you'll really appreciate this series of thoughtful deep dives on critically important topics like faith, the Bible, friendship, sexuality, philosophy, and more. As you engage with some world-class Christian scholars, you'll be encouraged, equipped, challenged, and above all invited to love God more with your heart, soul, mind, and strength."

—Andy Kim,
multiethnic resource director, InterVarsity Christian Fellowship

What Does Nature Teach Us about God?

Questions for Restless Minds

Questions for Restless Minds

QUESTIONS FOR RESTLESS MINDS

What Does Nature Teach Us about God?

Kirsten Birkett

D. A. Carson,
Series Editor

LEXHAM PRESS

What Does Nature Teach Us about God?
Questions for Restless Minds, edited by D. A. Carson

Print ISBN 9781683595090
Digital ISBN 9781683595106
Library of Congress Control Number 2021937694

Lexham Editorial: Todd Hains, Abigail Stocker, Mandi Newell
Cover Design: Brittany Schrock
Interior Design: Abigail Stocker
Typesetting: Justin Marr

The Christ on Campus Initiative exists to inspire students on college and university campuses to think wisely, act with conviction, and become more Christlike by providing relevant and excellent evangelical resources on contemporary issues.

Visit christoncampuscci.org.

Contents

Series Preface

D. A. CARSON, SERIES EDITOR

THE ORIGIN OF this series of books lies with a group of faculty from Trinity Evangelical Divinity School (TEDS), under the leadership of Scott Manetsch. We wanted to address topics faced by today's undergraduates, especially those from Christian homes and churches.

If you are one such student, you already know what we have in mind. You know that most churches, however encouraging they may be, are not equipped to prepare you for what you will face when you enroll at university.

It's not as if you've never known any winsome atheists before going to college; it's not as if you've never thought about Islam, or the credibility of the New Testament documents, or the nature of friendship, or gender identity, or how the claims of Jesus sound too exclusive and rather narrow, or the nature of evil. But up until now you've probably thought about such things within the shielding cocoon of a community of faith.

Now you are at college, and the communities in which you are embedded often find Christian perspectives to be at best oddly quaint and old-fashioned, if not repulsive. To use the current jargon, it's easy to become socialized into a new community, a new world.

How shall you respond? You could, of course, withdraw a little: just buckle down and study computer science or Roman history (or whatever your subject is) and refuse to engage with others. Or you could throw over your Christian heritage as something that belongs to your immature years and buy into the cultural package that surrounds you. Or—and this is what we hope you will do—you could become better informed.

But how shall you go about this? On any disputed topic, you do not have the time, and probably not the interest, to bury yourself in a couple of dozen volumes written by experts for experts. And if you did, that would be on *one* topic—and there are scores of topics that will grab the attention of the inquisitive student. On the other hand, brief pamphlets with predictable answers couched in safe slogans will prove to be neither attractive nor convincing.

So we have adopted a middle course. We have written short books pitched at undergraduates who want arguments that are accessible and stimulating, but invariably courteous. The material is comprehensive enough that it has become an important resource for pastors and other campus leaders who devote their energies to work with students. Each book ends with a brief annotated bibliography and study questions, intended for readers who want to probe a little further.

Lexham Press is making this series available both as attractive books and digitally in new formats (ebook and Logos resource). We hope and pray you will find them helpful and convincing.

1

INTRODUCTION

"**Y**ou," YOUR JOYS and your sorrows, your memories and your ambitions, your sense of personal identity and free will, are in fact no more than the behavior of a vast assembly of nerve cells and their associated molecules. ... A modern neurobiologist sees no need for the religious concept of a soul to explain the behavior of humans and other animals.[1]

I am attacking God, all gods, anything and everything supernatural, wherever and whenever they have been or will be invented.[2]

Whatever knowledge is attainable, must be attained by scientific methods; and what science cannot discover, mankind cannot know.[3]

I am a secular humanist. I think existence is what we make of it as individuals. There is no guarantee of life after death, and heaven and hell are what we created for ourselves, on this planet. There is no other home. Humanity originated here by evolution from lower forms over millions of years. And yes, I will speak plain, our ancestors were apelike animals. The human species has adapted physically and mentally to life on Earth and no place else. Ethics is the code of behavior we share on the basis of reason, law, honor, and an inborn sense of decency.[4]

One of the most common beliefs currently expounded in public literature is naturalism. Naturalism is a belief that only natural laws and forces work in the world. The supernatural (anything beyond the natural world, whether spiritual, magical or otherwise) does not exist. The physical universe is all that exists. Moreover, the only way to explain anything within the universe is in terms of entirely natural events and forces within the universe.[5]

Other terms that overlap with naturalism include materialism (the view that there is only matter, not souls, spirits, or deities) and atheism (the view that there is no God). Naturalism is not a new view. Indeed, some ancient Greek writings contain theories that matter is all that exists. Nonetheless, until very recently in history, it was a view that had very little widespread popularity. It is only in the last century or so that there has been a dramatic shift in public discourse, so that in most of the Western world today public literature generally assumes naturalism rather than otherwise. It is an even more recent phenomenon that atheism is fought for with a thoroughly religious fervor.[6]

Defenders of naturalism generally point to the successes of science to back up their worldview. Naturalism also assumes that the successes of science will eventually be absolute, that given enough time and effort, humans will be able to discover essentially everything about how the universe works. We are promised that in the near future there will probably be a Theory of Everything—not, despite its name, actually a theory of *everything*, but at least a theory that unifies all the fundamental forces of the universe. It is a grand claim, and the fact that such success in scientific discovery is indeed plausible is usually taken as support for naturalism rather than otherwise.[7]

However, despite its popularity, naturalism is a belief system with certain premises that must be assumed. It is not self-evident, nor is it a belief that convinced most people until recent times. How, then, have we come to this stage in history, when it is simply assumed true, without defense, in all sorts of publications? We need to understand a little of the history of ideas to understand how the present situation came about.[8]

2

HISTORY

As MENTIONED ABOVE, some of the ideas of naturalism go back to the ancient world, but we will pick up the story in the seventeenth century, where modern science has its roots. It was recognized at the time that explanations come in different types. We might ask, "Why does water boil?" One level of explanation would be that fire underneath the kettle makes the water hot. Another level would be that someone wanted to cook dinner. Both explanations give real causes for the boiling of the water, but the causes are of different types. This issue of understanding different levels of causation was very important in the early days of experimental science.[9]

FRANCIS BACON

Francis Bacon (1561–1626) was a philosopher. He was also a solicitor and politician who came to be Lord Chancellor of England, but it is his philosophical views that interest us here. One of his most important achievements was arguing that the best way to gain knowledge of the world was by the empirical method—that is, by making observations through experimentation. Bacon insisted that experimental science, or natural philosophy as it was called at the time, was the way forward. Not only did he advocate this as a philosophy, but he had very practical suggestions to make about the enterprise of science, including government-funded research, international communication through scientific journals, and collaboration in experimentation. Bacon was highly influential in starting what is now known as the Scientific Revolution in England.

Among other concerns, Bacon also wanted to reassure anyone who might have doubts that studying the natural world in no way suggested that God was being forgotten. God, he argued, was the first cause of everything. He is the ultimate reason that anything happens. God makes things happen, however, in certain natural ways. He makes flowers grow, for instance, by providing sunlight and rain. These mechanisms can be regarded as the secondary cause, the way in which God goes about doing things. By separating out first and second causes, Bacon was able to discuss the value of studying second causes while contemplating the first one.

> For certain it is that God worketh nothing in nature but by second causes: and if they would have it otherwise believed, it is mere imposture, as it were in favor towards God; and nothing else but to offer to the author of truth the unclean sacrifice of a lie. But further, it is an assured truth, and a conclusion of experience, that a little or superficial knowledge of philosophy may incline the mind of man to atheism, but a further proceeding therein doth bring the mind back again to religion. For in the entrance of philosophy, when the second causes, which are next

unto the senses, do offer themselves to the mind of man, if it dwell and stay there it may induce some oblivion of the highest cause; but when a man passeth on further, and seeth the dependence of causes, and the works of Providence, then, according to the allegory of the poets, he will easily believe that the highest link of nature's chain just needs be tied to the foot of Jupiter's chair. To conclude therefore, let no man upon a weak conceit of sobriety or an ill-applied moderation think or maintain, that a man can search too far, or be too well studied in the book of God's word, or in the book of God's works, divinity or philosophy; but rather let men endeavor an endless progress or proficience in both; only let men beware that they apply both to charity, and not to swelling; to use, and not to ostentation; and again, that they do not unwisely mingle or confound these learnings together.[10]

Science was to be a study of God's creation. In no way was it meant to replace belief in God. Bacon would have thought that ludicrous. Indeed, as we can see from the above quotation, he expected those who studied God's world to be equally well studied in God's word. The study of second causes was just that: a study of second causes, not a study of the only causes.

Francis Bacon turned out to be highly influential in the way that science came to be organized as a modern activity.

When the Royal Society of London was founded (still one of the leading scientific institutions in the world), its members consciously modeled their new society on Bacon's ideas. They took seriously his recommendations for establishing experimental, systematic science in order to expand human understanding and benefit humankind. They also took on his philosophical and theological background.

THE ROYAL SOCIETY

The Royal Society was set up in 1660 to study the natural world. That was the interest of its members. That was its charter. It was not to be a society for theological discussion. From the earliest days, then, there was general agreement. Whatever one wanted to do outside the meetings, the Royal Society met for the purpose of natural philosophy. The aim was to search into the secondary causes of things, to discover the mechanisms of how things worked in the world. It was not to matter whether the members were Puritans or Anglicans, a very important consideration given that the entire country had recently suffered civil war over that issue. "As for what belongs to the Members themselves, that are to constituted the Society: It is to be noted, that they have freely admitted Men of different Religions, Countries and Professions of Life."[11] Theology was not to be a topic of discussion: the members of the society "meddle no otherwise with Divine things, than only as the Power, and Wisdom, and Goodness of the Creator, is display'd in the admirable order and workmanship of the Creatures."[12]

As the latter part of this quotation reveals, the decision not to discuss theology was hardly because of atheism. On the contrary, although members might differ about church politics, they would have considered themselves Christians. It was typical of their scientific publications to talk overtly of God and that they were bringing about a better understanding of the glory of God's handiwork. Their focus, however, was on the created things, even if they never forgot the creator, and in practice it was better to restrict their discussions to theories of mechanism rather than politically touchy subjects that theological discussion could easily arouse.

In other words, the Royal Society was going to study (in Bacon's terms) secondary causes, not first causes. It was assumed that God did things in ways that did not involve frequent miracles but in ways that would proceed in an orderly and understandable fashion. The secondary causes, then, were the ones open to experimentation.[13]

This should have been a straightforward matter. There is nothing in investigating God's secondary means of doing things that provides any rivalry to God as the origin of all action. Certainly most of the famous scientific writings of the time, and for more than a century later, gave clear recognition to God as the one who actually made the things that science was investigating. Another writer from the seventeenth century, however, might have been able to give a warning.

WILLIAM PERKINS

William Perkins (1558–1602) is hardly heard of these days, being one of those much maligned individuals known as the Puritans, but in his time he was a widely published author and popular preacher at Cambridge. He was not a scientist, nor did he write much on the natural world. However he was against superstition, and in one work he argued that astrology is a waste of time. Students interested in astrology should rather employ themselves studying God's real works, not imagined things like astrological influence.

Even in his time, however, Perkins was well aware of what might happen when enthusiastic students started thinking that understanding the natural world was all they needed to know.

> This thy dealing is like unto the folly of that man, who having a costly clock in his home, never extolleth or thinketh on the wit and invention of the clockmaker, but is continually in admiration of the spring or watch of the clocke, by whose means all the wheels have their swifter or slower, their backward or forward motions, and by which the whole clock keeps its course. Wherefore I think that in a Christian commonwealth, those only books should

> be published for thine use, which might beat into
> thine head, and make thee every hour and moment
> to think on the providence of God: which being once
> settled in thy mind, the consideration of the means,
> which God useth, will follow of itself. Contrarywise,
> to tell thee the means which God doth use, to thun-
> der out the aspects and constellations of Stars, and
> seldom to mention of his providence, maketh thee
> to fear, and admire, and love the means, quite for-
> getting the work of God in the means.[14]

It was a timely warning. It is an excellent thing to study the
works of God. Even non-scientists such as Perkins warmly
recommended it. Nonetheless, he knew the tendency of
human hearts. It is all too easy to become so enchanted
with the means that God uses to forget that it is God who
is using them.

WILLIAM PALEY

For many throughout the eighteenth and nineteenth centuries, Perkins's warning might have seemed utterly unnecessary. Virtually no one with any intellectual credibility
doubted God. Certainly the study of the natural world was
no reason for doing so. On the contrary, the workings of
the natural world were taken as one of the most convincing
reasons to believe in a creator God. This was the premise of
a highly influential book written in the eighteenth century
that served as a university text well into the nineteenth:

Natural Theology by the English theologian William Paley (1743–1805).

Paley's work might be seen as a grand argument for the reality of first causes. His argument was that God's hand was seen clearly in the design apparent in nature. We can know that nature is the work of God because each detail is so carefully crafted to fit its end. Again, we find the example of clockwork (in this case, a watch):

In crossing a heath, suppose I pitched my foot against a stone and were asked how the stone came to be there, I might possibly answer that for anything I knew to the contrary it had lain there forever; nor would it, perhaps, be very easy to show the absurdity of this answer. But suppose I had found a watch upon the ground, and it should be inquired how the watch happened to be in that place, I should hardly think of the answer which I had before given, that for anything I knew the watch might have always been there. Yet why should not this answer serve for the watch as well as for the stone? Why is it not as admissible in the second case as in the first? For this reason, and for no other, namely, that when we come to inspect the watch, we perceive—what we could not discover in the stone—that its several parts are framed and put together for a purpose, e.g., that they are so formed and adjusted as to produce motion, and that motion so regulated as to point out the hour of the day; that if the different parts had been differently shaped from what they are, of a different size from what they are, or placed after any other manner or in any other order than that in which they are placed, either no motion at all would have been carried on in the machine, or none which would have answered the use that is now served by it. ... This mechanism being observed—it requires indeed an examination of the instrument, and perhaps some previous knowledge of the subject, to perceive and understand it; but being once, as we have said, observed and understood—the inference we think is inevitable, that the watch must have had a maker—that there must have existed, at some time and at some place or other, an artificer or artificers who formed it for the purpose which we find it actually to answer, who comprehended its construction and designed its use.[15]

The argument is simple: if you find a watch, it is obvious that someone made the watch. Paley will go on to argue that all sorts of things in the natural world are just as complex and as intricate as a watch. We should, therefore, conclude that the natural world also had a maker.

This sounds a lot like Perkins's argument about the clock. However, there is a major difference. For Perkins knew perfectly well that the natural world is God's creation. He did not need to study it in order to find out; he knew because the Bible had told him. Paley's work, on the other hand, is operating from a different premise. He argues in the opposite direction: we know that there is a creator by reason of the intricacy of creation. Instead of the creator explaining the creation, the argument is now being used the other way around. We are being asked to believe in the creator because of creation because there is no other suitable explanation.[16]

Let us put this in terms of Bacon's first and secondary causes. Paley argued that God's existence is more probable, given the way the world works. That is, secondary causes on their own are not sufficient to explain the world as it is. One needs first causes as well. In Paley's day, this was generally considered a very strong argument. It did seem inexplicable that the living world could contain such intricate and interdependent structures unless a designer God had made it that way. This is precisely what a young student, studying to be a clergyman at Cambridge in the 1820s, thought of Paley's work: "I did not at the time trouble myself about Paley's premises; and taking these on trust, I was charmed and convinced by the long line of argumentation."[17]

The problem with an argument for God's existence based on the intricacy of the natural world is that it depends on the human's evaluation of how good the secondary causes are. If a human viewer decides that, actually, the secondary causes look pretty convincing on their own, then that person may well decide that there is no need for a first cause. The "first cause" becomes not a cause at all, but an unnecessary speculation.[18]

With William Paley, scientific theism was alive and well. It might seem that God was firmly part of the understanding of the natural world. Paley's argument, however, effectively restricted and reduced the role that the creator was understood to have. What is a true statement of the Bible (God has created a world in which parts work together ingeniously) was turned around into an argument (we know God exists because we can observe a world in which parts work together ingeniously). This was then promoted, in many people's minds, to a single, knockdown argument (the main, perhaps the only, reason we know God exists is that we can observe a world in which parts work together ingeniously), and it set up God, not as the known creator, but as an explanatory theory. This was not what Paley intended, but it was the way many people took the argument and the way many restate it now.[19] In this sense, Paley set up the challenge that there is no other way to explain a world in which parts work together ingeniously, except by the deliberate design of a creator God.

The stage was set for Charles Darwin. He was the Cambridge theology student mentioned above who at first was totally convinced by Paley's argument. He was also to be the one who provided an alternative explanation for the evidence of apparent design that Paley had described so carefully. His account of secondary causes would come to be seen as so thorough and complete that, for many people, there was no longer a need for a first cause at all.

CHARLES DARWIN

The young Charles Darwin (1809–1882) studied Paley's work at Cambridge when undertaking study for ordination in the Church of England. He found Paley's argument convincing. It would seem that, like much of nineteenth-century British society, it was the chief foundation on which he rested his belief in God and in the truth of Christianity.

For Darwin himself and for countless others to follow, to find a mechanism by which nature could come to be organized to the benefit of living organisms was a deadly threat to his Christianity. That mechanism is precisely what Darwin is so famous for discovering.

> If during the long course of ages and under varying conditions of life, organic beings vary at all in the several parts of their organization, and I think this cannot be disputed; if there be, owing to the high geometrical powers of increase of each species, at some age, season, or year, a severe struggle for life, and this certainly cannot be disputed; then, considering the infinite complexity of the relations of all organic beings to each other and to their conditions of existence, causing an infinite diversity in structure, constitution, and habits, to be advantageous to them,

I think it would be a most extraordinary fact if no variation ever had occurred useful to each being's own welfare, in the same way as so many variations have occurred useful to man. But if variations useful to any organic being do occur, assuredly individuals thus characterized will have the best chance of being preserved in the struggle for life; and from the strong principle of inheritance they will tend to produce offspring similarly characterized. This principle of preservation, I have called, for the sake of brevity, Natural Selection.[20]

Darwin speculated that the reason living organisms seem to be so superbly adapted to their natural environments, all the parts working together so well, was not because this was the immediate work of a Designer. On the contrary, there was a natural explanation: it was a result of natural selection. Paley's challenge had been met.

This, to Darwin, was the end of his belief in a creator God. "The old argument from design in Nature, as given by Paley, which formerly seemed to me so conclusive, fails, now that the law of natural selection has been discovered."[21] Darwin had believed in God, not as the first cause who worked through many ingenious secondary causes, but as the conclusion of an argument based on what was observed in nature. Having set up God in his mind as an explanatory theory, the discovery of what he saw as an alternative explanation crushed the only role he had for God.

It was a source of great personal sadness for Charles Darwin. On the other hand, men like Thomas Henry Huxley ("Darwin's bulldog") hailed it as a triumph because they wished to see God deleted from the scene anyway. Eager to use any means at hand to fight his political battles on behalf of naturalism, Huxley was delighted with Darwin's theory, even though he was not at all convinced that it was true. The theory had something far more important going for it than scientific truth; it provided him with a non-theistic account of nature.

THOMAS HUXLEY

Huxley (1825–1895) was a scientist with a passionate devotion to science as a philosophy. He had a vision for English society: to see men of science recognized as the true intellectual leaders of society and scientific education improved to the point where science could take pride of place as a profession. This meant more than just improving the career-paths of professional scientists. Huxley wanted naturalistic philosophy to take the place of Christianity as the ruling philosophy of society. He wanted scientific thinking and scientific leaders to replace religious thinking and religious leaders, who were simply in the way of society.[22]

To understand Huxley's aims, we must recognize certain characteristics of English society at the time. While a lot of scientific study was being done, it was not a professional career as it is now. To a large extent, science was done by wealthy gentlemen who could afford to fund their own research. To become a member of the Royal Society, social class was more important than technical expertise or published research. Many members of the Royal Society no doubt regarded it as a hobby, an interesting pursuit in one's spare time.[23]

Nor was there any such thing as a degree in science as we would think of it now. University education was largely based on the classics with any scientific classes being elective extras. In general, university education was dominated by the Church of England, and a great many of those who actually engaged in the practice of science, especially botany and geology, were clergy. Class, and the spare time and wealth it brought, were far more important in pursuing science than actual education.

Charles Darwin had originally seen his life developing along these lines. Before he went on his famous voyage on the *Beagle*, he had intended to become a country clergyman, filling his hours mostly with observation of nature and careful recording of his findings. It was a common and respectable pursuit for a gentleman. Likewise, when Darwin finally published his theory, the public looked to church leaders to comment on its scientific quality. Church leaders were the kind of well-read, intellectual thinkers who would be naturally expected to give an expert opinion on the matter.

Thomas Huxley, however, thoroughly disliked this organization of society. He was personally against the Church of England, and in fact against religion in general. In particular, he hated the idea that religious leaders were regarded as having the right to comment on intellectual issues. As someone who had to earn his own living, he also resented the fact that science was not a paying pursuit. He wrote to his fiancée in 1851,

> To attempt to live by any scientific pursuit is a farce. ... A man of science may earn great distinction, but not bread. He will get enough invitations to all sorts of dinners and conversations, but not enough income to pay a cab.[24]

Huxley did not want science dominated by the landed gentry. He wanted it to be led by men such as himself: professional men, particularly non-theists, devoted to science as a living.

Huxley was ambitious and energetic, an excellent organizer and public speaker. He and a group of allies set about changing British society by taking control of the scientific institutions and seeking to change the way both scientific education and scientific influence were organized. He aimed for an incredible achievement, and it is even more incredible that to a great extent he succeeded.

Through sheer force of perseverance, as well as considerable expertise in behind-the-scenes political engineering, Huxley and his small group of scientific friends managed to take over control of science in England. Calling themselves the "X-club," Huxley and eight other men would meet for dinner just before the meetings of the Royal Society. They would discuss suitable candidates for positions of influence in various scientific bodies and how to have them appointed or elected. From 1873 to 1885, every president of the Royal Society was a member of the X-club, so their discussions were extraordinarily fruitful. All over Britain, prominent scientific societies came to be dominated by X-club members or their friends.[25]

At the same time, Huxley was becoming more and more famous as a public commentator on science. This was another part of the battle. Huxley wanted not just for professional and atheistic men of science like himself to be in charge of scientific institutions; he wanted them to be recognized publicly as the dominant intellectuals of society. In his view, naturalism must take over the role of Christianity as the dominant philosophy. This was more than a battle of political influence; it was a battle over what was to be the public definition of truth. Huxley wanted naturalism to be the default position of public discourse. He did not want theologians to have a right to give public opinions; that right was to be restricted to scientific thinkers, without theism having any part in it. In a lecture in 1866, he outlined what he thought would be the future of science and scientific thinking:

> If these ideas be destined, as I believe they are, to
> be more and more firmly established as the world
> grows older; if that spirit be fated, as I believe it
> is, to extend itself into all departments of human

thought, and to become co-extensive with the range of knowledge; if, as our race approaches its maturity, it discovers, as I believe it will, that there is but one kind of knowledge and but one method of acquiring it; then we, who are still children, may justly feel it our highest duty to recognize the advisableness of improving natural knowledge, and so to aid ourselves and our successors in our course toward the noble goal which lies before mankind.[26]

Religion, if not to be abolished altogether, was to be made a private matter of emotion and values—not something that deserved any place in serious intellectual discussion. Instead, all the deference and respect previously given to religion in society was to come to science, to the "church scientific" (as Huxley called it); himself the bishop who gave "lay sermons" in the form of scientific lectures. Huxley even wrote to one friend in 1871 that he was giving lectures in biology to schoolmasters "with a view of converting them into scientific missionaries to convert the Christian Heathen of these islands to the true faith."[27]

In other words, Huxley wanted far more than respect for science as a profession. This was part of the battle, of course. Huxley and his friends constantly publicized the successes of science and the improvements in industry that resulted. Such successes were very well-received in the atmosphere of progress that dominated the nineteenth century. Yet more than that, Huxley managed to have this success attributed to the naturalistic philosophy in general. It was not a fair attribution. By far the majority of those actually working in science and industry would probably have thought of themselves as Christian and would have been appalled at the thought of atheism. That was irrelevant. Huxley, in the way he presented the successes of science, consistently allied them with a naturalistic worldview, giving the impression that it was only a non-theistic philosophy that could guarantee social progress.

Indeed, one of Huxley's favorite techniques was to set science and theology up as rivals, with science as the inevitable victor. Time after time he would portray science in mythical terms as the hero, striving forward against adversity and ultimately victorious, while religion was the villain, trying to stop progress but unable to do so.

> Extinguished theologians lie about the cradle of every science as the strangled snakes beside that of Hercules; and history records that whenever science and orthodoxy have been fairly opposed, the latter has been forced to retire from the lists, bleeding and crushed, if not annihilated; scotched, if not slain.[28]

Huxley was a very capable speaker and popular writer. His point of view was persuasively stated and generally successful in swaying public opinion. Moreover, he was indefatigable. His output was prodigious. Through sheer force of repetition, constant publicity, and forceful presentation,

Huxley managed to take society with him. People began to believe his message that science was necessarily anti-religious and was better than religion. Due to the efforts of popularists like Huxley, people began to believe that Darwin had, indeed, provided the means to become an intellectually fulfilled atheist.[29]

SUMMARY

Let us sum up our story so far.

There was a time when to question the existence of God in educated society was ludicrous. In particular, to see science as anything other than discovering the handiwork of God was not really even considered. Science was done for the glory of God and to uncover the excellence of God's craftsmanship. This was so obvious a statement that it was taken for granted.

Humans are perverse creatures, however, and as the intellectual history of the last few centuries shows, the more we discovered about the details of God's excellence in creation, the more we failed to focus on the one who actually deserves the glory for these discoveries. The more impressed we become with the cleverness of "science" to uncover truth, the more we forget the cleverness of the person who actually provided the truth to uncover. William Perkins, that humble Puritan writing so many centuries ago, prophesied truly.

This did not happen as part of a simple process from theism to atheism in understanding the world. The public shift in this direction came partly from misunderstanding the Bible, and largely from the propaganda of determined atheists who capitalized on this misunderstanding and managed to sway public opinion successfully. The pragmatic decision, taken so long ago, to leave first causes out of science has seeped through to become an (unjustified) absolute.

Nonetheless, does this tell us anything other than a nice historical story? Regardless of how people came to dismiss God in favor on naturalism, maybe it was the right thing to do. Surely, these days, science has proved there is no need for God?

SCIENCE AND
NATURALISM TODAY

Science today is thoroughly naturalistic. Any movements to the contrary are fervently and noisily resisted. The supernatural, we are told most firmly, has no place in science.

For practical reasons, it may make sense for scientists to talk about natural causes only, for natural causes are what they are interested in. What does not make sense is to turn this into an argument that claims that science therefore proves that natural causes are the only ones.

In fact it is almost tautological to say this. Science cannot incorporate supernatural phenomena, for whatever science can study and analyze is defined as natural. For instance, magnetism was once thought of as an occult force, but in becoming analyzable and quantifiable, in coming under the aegis of science, it came to be thought of as natural. In the nineteenth century it became very popular to try to verify the existence of spirits scientifically. People would set up a scientific apparatus to try to detect changes in electricity or such things in an effort to find scientific evidence for these phenomena. If they had found such evidence, however, the thing would now be an object of scientific study. It would be part of the "real" world that science studies. It is no longer supernatural. It is just another, albeit bizarre, phenomenon of the world. If there is scientific evidence for something, then it is something in this world, and it is studied as natural.

Whatever is supernatural, if it is genuinely supernatural (i.e., beyond this world), then it is not able to be studied by the activity that studies this world. Science is unable to disprove the spiritual, for if the spiritual agency does something in this world, then the evidence for the spiritual agency is precisely the evidence for what is defined as a natural activity. Whatever science discovers is natural. This is not an argument. It is a matter of definition.

It is time, then, for us to consider what science is by definition and practice.

3

WHAT IS
SCIENCE?

. . . . .

W HAT CONSTITUTES A scientific explanation?[30] What are the criteria by which we judge something to be scientific—indeed what, precisely, is science?

This becomes an important issue at these controversial points where some see science as having reached its limits. In 1997 the cosmologist Lee Smolin presented a theory of an infinite series of universes. He was criticized because his theory about the beginnings of the universe was not science, but rather metaphysics, because it was not testable. Smolin, on the other hand, insisted that it was "speculative science."[31]

What makes a theory scientific? How do we tell?

The word "science" is not a simple one. It is used with many different meanings, and often we find meanings sliding between contexts, so a legitimate use in one context is taken illegitimately in another. For instance, science got us to the moon, so science works. Science gives the best answers to the deep questions of life—better than religion, which never got anyone to the moon. Science is what rational people should believe, not religion.

In what sense, however, did science get us to the moon? In this statement, the word "science" is referring to a number of things. A large group of highly-trained people who had been provided with an immense amount of money used mathematical calculations to predict where the moon would be relative to the earth at a certain time and how a spaceship should move in order to arrive there. They also used experimentally elicited information about metals (their stresses and capacities) and fuels (the propulsion they provide and the rate at which they burn) to engineer a spaceship that would survive the trip. In time, this project was successful, and the spaceship arrived at the moon as planned.

We can accept that this was a highly successful enterprise. It did what it set out to do, and we can agree that the problem was a very difficult one. The stated aim was achieved. If it was science that did this, then science worked very well.

Now what relevance does this have to accepting a scientific explanation of the universe over a religious one? When science is spoken of as explaining life, the universe, and everything, we are no longer talking about a particular technical triumph. By a scientific explanation of the universe, people mean one which does not use God as part of the explanation of how the universe, or we, came to be here. It means an explanation that is entirely naturalistic, with no sense of purpose or intelligent intention. This is a philosophical position—if you like, a metaphysical one. This meaning of "science" in "science explains the universe" is very different from the meaning of "science" in "science got us to the moon." But we have experienced a clever slide of meaning here. The science that got us to the moon was very successful in its own terms, and this success is transferred over to the science that gives an explanation of the universe. But naturalistic philosophy has not displayed the kind of success that moon-going calculations did. It does not deserve the attribution of success that moon-goingness does. The kind of success that the moon project achieved is almost entirely irrelevant to a philosophy that aims to explain the universe naturalistically. It is an entirely different kind of project.

We need to be more careful about using and understanding these terms. We will try, then, to tease out some of the different ways in which science is understood. This has an even deeper level of complexity, for not only is the word used in different ways in common language, but ever since science began there has been an ongoing philosophical debate about what the definition of science should be. This debate has continued up to the present, as some of the traditionally accepted meanings of science have come under close scrutiny. We will try to interweave these two discussions by looking at the different ways in which the word science is understood and then at some of the debates over that particular aspect of science.

THE METHOD OF SCIENCE

What is science? At first glance, it should be easy to define. It is what scientists do in laboratories, wearing white coats, carrying test-tubes around. It is experiments, testing hypotheses and theories to see if the results are what the theory predicts. It is the whole industry of people delving into the natural world, studying it, experimenting on it, observing it, and coming to verifiable conclusions about what the world is and does.

It does not take much investigation into the practice of science, however, to start to be a little confused about what it actually involves. A scientist could be a person who follows tornados around and records wind speeds, goes to the bottom of the ocean in a highly pressurized diving unit, or never does anything more adventurous than look at a computer in an office. The theories a scientist works with could be chemical formulae, mathematical functions, or descriptions of prehistoric artifacts. They might concern times in the long distant past or billions of years into the future. A scientist might work on the scale of the subatomic or the galactic, with the digestion of an ant, the mating behavior of a buffalo, or the rate of change of a forest. Would an observer from another planet easily group all these studies into the one category? In what sense are all these different activities the same thing?

If the objects of study, the kind of theories, or the scale of investigation cannot be the thing that binds together all these activities, in an important sense the *method* of investigation can. Science still, essentially, works on the same principles described by Bacon centuries ago. What unifies all the different practices that go under the heading "science" is that its discoveries are meant to be based on collecting empirical data from the world. Once data are collected and analyzed, then theories can be pursued that might predict new ways of understanding how the world works. It is assumed that there will be widespread regularities that will explain on a general level what happens in the particular circumstance.[32]

In some issues, this is a relatively straightforward matter. What is the structure of an atom? At one time, atoms were thought to be solid and have no smaller parts. Through experimentation, that theory was shown to be false, and gradually a picture of an atom containing a nucleus with an orbit of electrons was developed. In time, after further experimentation, that picture was also discovered to be too simple, and much smaller parts again were discovered within the nucleus. Through a process of experimenting, theorizing, testing, and more theorizing, more and more things were and still are being discovered about the structure of matter.

For other areas of scientific study, however, it can be much more difficult to come to agreement about the proper scientific conclusions to be drawn. It can be very difficult to isolate which factors are the relevant ones that need to be studied, especially when things like human politics are affected by scientific conclusions.

To pick a currently contentious issue, it is observed that over time the average temperature of the earth is rising. That observation is based on data gathered in many different ways such as measurements from the atmosphere and oceans, from studying ice cores for changes in the way ice has formed over centuries, and even human records from past times. The observation part of science is painstaking and detailed. Any conclusion that the earth's temperature is rising must be based on many, many observations in all sorts of different conditions. Only then can the conclusion be regarded as reliable.

What, however, explains the rise in temperature? That is another issue again. One theory is that human production of carbon dioxide, pumped into the atmosphere, causes global warming. Another theory is that the earth naturally goes through cycles of heating and cooling and that we just happen to be in a heating phase at the moment. Which of these theories we take to be true will have massive implications for public policy about energy production. If human activity is responsible for the rise in temperature, then we are in grave danger that the more we act in the same way, the further the temperature will rise to the detriment of us all. If, on the other hand, we are simply going through a natural cycle and human activity has nothing to do with it, then we need not worry; the cycle will reverse again in time, and the earth will cool.

When a theory can have massive effect on whole industries, a great deal of pressure is placed on science to come up with a definitive answer. This goes against the nature of most scientific inquiry, which is slow, painstaking, and careful, gathering information and testing it within strict limits. The whole world system can hardly be tested in a laboratory. It is a very complex matter with a huge number of variables. Conclusions must be drawn with great care.

It can be very frustrating for policy-makers that science works this way, but making sure that conclusions are strictly drawn from evidence is the very strength of science.

Science, then, at its most basic is a method for finding out how the world works. It is based on certain principles that inspire confidence in the knowledge it produces. It depends upon actual observations, noted, tested, repeated, and confirmed. It requires tests to be repeatable by other people in different conditions. Scientific conclusions are not meant to be based on the secret observations of one individual or on isolated opinions. Science is based on the idea that we can, in principle, work out knowledge that is objective because it is observed by many different people and tested in multiple ways. For many, that kind of knowledge is the only knowledge worth having. It is trustworthy precisely because it does not depend on who a person is, but how they carry out their task.

But can we be sure? How can we know that this way of understanding the world is reliable? Ever since science began as an activity, there has been a parallel field of inquiry that keeps asking such questions. We put a lot of trust in science in our modern, Western world, and the fact of our advances in technology seems to justify that trust. But how can we be sure? Throughout the eighteenth and nineteenth centuries, philosophers have pondered these questions because even if observations are made carefully and painstakingly, there is still the risk of error and uncertainty. Moreover, in principle there still remain certain insurmountable problems in being sure that empirical science is the way to true knowledge.

David Hume, for instance, pointed out the problem of induction: you may be able to frame general laws from multiple instances of something, but you can never be sure that the next instance will not contradict your law. Immanuel Kant proposed that we can never know for sure that our senses are telling us what the world is actually like, for all our sense data are necessarily "filtered" by the innate categories of thought we have in our minds. Despite this, however, science could still be held to be progressively approaching truth. For instance, William Whewell (who coined the word "scientist" to replace "natural philosopher") claimed that confidence in science was justified on the grounds that disparate laws in separate fields could come to be explained by the one overarching law, just as Newton's theory of gravitation had explained such separate things as the motion of planets and the tides on earth.[33]

The problem is, every time we try to tie down what it is that makes science a reliable way to find certain knowledge, problems crop up. The idea that science makes observations, then inductively constructs theories, and then tests the theories has difficulties at each of those points.

ONE RESPONSE: FALSIFIABILITY

The philosopher Karl Popper (1902–1994) was one who sought to distinguish carefully what it was that made something scientific, and his solution has been widely quoted in scientific literature.[34]

Popper was struck by the way in which Einsteinian physics, a radically new theory that challenged the old, made extremely precise and "risky" predictions, such as that light from stars would be bent by the gravitational attraction of the sun, something that could be tested during a solar eclipse. This was tested in 1919, and the prediction made from the theory of general relativity was confirmed. This, to Popper, seemed to be something qualitatively different from, say, Freudian psychoanalysis which explained things only "after the fact," not making risky predictions. It is easy to find confirmations of a theory if you make the theory all-encompassing enough. Confirmations mean something only if the prediction was unlikely or risky. There has to be a chance that the prediction be incorrect for the confirmation to be worth anything. Only if the prediction might not have come true is the theory being genuinely tested. What matters is not just that the theory is confirmed, but that it be in principle falsifiable. So Popper came to his famous conclusion that what makes a theory scientific is its falsifiability, refutability, or testability.

This general view has a lot of power, and Popper's work has been condensed to a slogan of "falsifiability" which has appealed to many people as a good description of the essence of science. Whatever your field is—whether astronomy, biology, or archaeology—the important thing is that your theories should be such that they can be tested by the data. The real world must have the last say. Unfortunately, it is in the very practice of science that this description starts to falter. The problem is, scientists often do not just accept what the data say. In practice, what do you do if the experiment fails? Does this really prove your theory was wrong? Or was your experimental technique wrong? Or was the equipment faulty? Or was one of the auxiliary hypotheses wrong? For instance, if the experiment on Einstein's theory had shown no bending of light around the sun, would this have proved Einstein wrong or the theory of optics on which the measuring equipment was based? It is possible to stay with a theory even if the experimental data are going against it at the moment, for the theory may have other strengths such as its coherence within the mathematical framework or its overall explanatory power.

THE PROBLEM OF
EMPIRICAL EQUIVALENCE

Despite the logical flaws we can now see with these definitions of science, the idea that science is reliable because it is tested against data is still a very powerful one. If there are two competing theories, we test them to see which one makes the correct predictions. So when Galileo looked through his telescope at the moons of Jupiter, he was testing two theories: one that says everything revolves around the Earth and his own theory that denied this. The moons of Jupiter were seen to revolve around Jupiter, not Earth, so Galileo claimed his theory was a better one than the old. This way of determining between theories seems self-evident to us: see which one works.

Nevertheless, this idea of testing theories to verify them assumes that the theories make different predictions. What if there are two theories that are equally elegant and equally explain the data but make the same predictions? How can you tell which one is true? When the method rests on testing predictions against empirical data, there is no way of determining between them. You can only hope that one day, with further research, some situation will arise in which the two theories will make different predictions. However, this raises another problem for faith in science. If there is only one existing theory whose predictions fare well against tested data, how can you be sure that there is not another equally good (or better) one that has not yet been thought of? Science is limited by the ingenuity of scientists. If no one has thought of the true theory, then no one knows the truth. How can we ever be sure that the true theory is not yet discovered? How can we be sure that someone will think of it?[35]

The more confirming evidence there is, the more confident we can be that a theory is a good one, but it still might be wrong. Scientific theories come and go. Many scientific theories were successful in their day (i.e., they explained the observable phenomena and made confirmed predictions) but have been discarded. Medieval astronomy held that there were crystalline spheres carrying the planets around the earth. Medicine used to be based on four "humors," the right balance of which ensured good health. Chemistry used to include a substance called "phlogiston,"

45

whose effects are now explained by oxygen. Heat gain or loss was explained by a gain or loss of "caloric," now thought not to exist. Electromagnetic waves were thought to move through the "aether." Because most people are not very well educated in the history of science (or only know of its heroic "successes"), it is easy to lose sight of just how often scientific theories have changed. There is little, if anything, of the great discoveries of the scientific revolution that still survive unchanged. Science is always revisable, and it is very frequently revised. It is because science can always be revised in the light of new data that we have any confidence in it at all.[36]

Until we know everything in the universe, we will not know whether our science is right. What is more, given our current limitations as human beings, we would not know if we knew everything in the universe. We could not be sure there was not more to know. As things stand now, the very way in which science proceeds (i.e., by testing theories against observational data) limits the amount we can know from science. There may always be something else we have not yet thought of.

SCIENCE AND COMMUNITY

We have examined the most basic and common understanding of how to define "science": science is an empirical method of studying the world. But there is another definition: science is the people who do it. This may sound strange. Surely we should say that "scientists" is the word for the people who do it? That is true, but it is also a common usage for "science" to mean the people, too. Take for instance the simple phrase "science proves." This is an odd phrase, for what is the subject that is doing the proving? It has to be a person or a group of people. Science does not prove anything; people do. If we are going to understand what "science" is, we must take into account that people do it.

Doing this, however, complicates the picture somewhat. When we move from purely methodological descriptions of what science "is" or "ought to be" to the real world of what scientists actually do, the picture becomes somewhat more messy. The world of science is not a matter of obedient robots going about following logical rules. It is a world of real people who can be creative or dull, law-abiding or unruly, innovative or boring, honest or dishonest, career-minded or dedicated to the pure pursuit of knowledge, and often all of these at different times. Whatever may be the logical niceties of scientific methodology, they are embodied in an industry of funded research, peer review, and journal publication. Working scientists have many complaints about their system. Peer review can put the fate of your research into the hands of a rival. The science that succeeds has to be first of all the science that is funded, and that itself is often decided by people with vested interests. Young scientists find it hard to get jobs, old scientists hoard power, and everyone complains about the facilities.

It was by comparing traditional theories of science with the real world of how scientific discoveries have happened that several theorists took a new approach to the philosophy of science.[37] It is not appropriate, they said, to write about the "logic" of theories, as if they exist as complete, formulated entities. Theories develop in a process of trial and error, intuitive leaps, discussion, and thought within a scientific community. Instead of looking at scientific theories in the abstract and trying to work out what the ideal theory "should" be, philosophers of science should instead be looking at the way scientists interact and come to new ideas, how their training affects their conclusions, and so on.

Pushing this to the limits, there has been of recent years a strand of philosophy of science that has focused on the sociological dimension of science. Some writers have concluded that science does not really deserve to make claims about "truth," given what a thoroughly human and political enterprise it is. It is not just the darker side of human nature that promotes such skepticism about the reliability of scientific knowledge. Further investigation into science in practice can be confusing when it comes to establishing the criteria for truth. The difficulty in establishing certainty in scientific practice has led some authors to the extremes of denying that scientific knowledge is "knowledge" in the generally accepted sense at all. Rather, it is merely a social construction. A "fact," then, is simply a statement that enough important people agree upon.

The most radical skeptical theories about science are not generally accepted. Between the two extremes (naive acceptance that science reveals facts that can be proved true on one side and total relativism on the other) we need to find a reasonable account of science. Science works on a day-to-day basis in a very organized, orderly, and rational manner. Results are tested against new data, and theories are subject to independent verification. What is the point, then, of recognizing the social aspect of science? It is that in order to test results at all, criteria must be set up that decide what constitutes a reasonable test. When theories are tested against data, someone has to decide which data are relevant. Someone has to decide which kinds of results are the most important. In the end, just saying "it works" is not good enough. It works in what context? Ptolemaic astronomy, which assumed stars, planets, and the sun revolved around the earth, worked very well for drawing up navigational charts. It accurately predicted positions of the planets and events like eclipses. When the theory was overthrown, it was not because the new one worked better in these ways. Rather, new criteria (for example, mathematical simplicity) had become important.

Science does work, given these sensible qualifications of what "work" means. It works not just in its technological applications, but in gathering a remarkably complex, comprehensive and interlocking way of understanding the universe. Science achieves what western civilization wants it to achieve. What the analysis of scientific epistemology does teach us is that to claim that science can give us certain knowledge about everything, as popular rhetoric has claimed since the seventeenth century, is rather overstating the case. We must get away from naive statements that science "proves" this or that. It is not just overambitious but practically foolhardy to expect absolute certain proof of theories. Scientific conclusions are always tentative and revisable. This is the very strength of science.

For in keeping its theories tentative and revisable, science is able to retain some hope of discovering something about reality. It is not the grand claim of certain knowledge. It is a much more limited ambition, which many working scientists share. Science is a practical method for finding things out that involves hunches, rule-of-thumb heuristics, and training in the craft of research. It has its flaws, but as a general way of proceeding, it works rather well.

SUMMARY

Let us again sum up the story so far.

A popular philosophy today insists that the natural world is all there is. There is no God or supernatural forces at work. One of the strongest supports for this philosophy, it is claimed, is science. Science gives us full explanations for the workings of the universe, and we have no need for any further explanation.

We have seen, however, that this very argument is flawed. Science does not and cannot explain the whole universe. It is a valuable and largely reliable method for uncovering the mechanisms of the physical world. Within certain limits, it is very powerful. It is not, however, infallible and certainly not the basis for all knowledge.

Moreover, God is not simply an alternative explanation for the same things that science explains. He is the one who created the universe that science explains. Science is the practice of studying the secondary causes of things, the mechanism by which God makes them happen. Science is no magic wand. It is an enterprise that has been very successful, for all its flaws, at understanding the way in which the universe works. It does not, however, and cannot give ultimate explanations for why things are the way they are.

We can go further than that. It is only because the universe was created by God that science is possible at all. We are able to study and understand the universe because God created it. Science does not dismiss the need for God. On the contrary, science is possible only because of God.

That is a bold statement that does not sit well with certain modern sensibilities. There are certain prerequisites, however, before science is possible at all. There needs to be some grounds, for instance, for assuming that there *is* an objective reality for science to study and that it is *not* simply a matter of political construction. We also need some grounds for establishing that real knowledge of this universe is possible. This is necessary to overcome Hume's objections about observations and to have confidence that what we have consistently observed to be true in the past will remain true.

In other words, science needs a firm foundation in order to have reason to overcome these real philosophical problems. That science, on the whole, "works," is something, but not enough. Why does it work? Why is it that humans, insignificant, prone to mistakes, and difficult to get along with as we are, can be successful in science at all? There are answers to these questions, but they are not found in naturalism. Contrary to the dearly held beliefs of some, the best basis for believing in science is found in the Bible.

To understand that, we need to know a little more about what the Bible says about God and this universe he has created.

4

THE BIBLE AND THE NATURAL WORLD

T HE FIRST VERSE of the Bible says, "In the beginning God created the heavens and earth" (Gen 1:1). It is the first and most basic truth of the Bible.

Plato would have it that the original maker molded the universe from pre-existing matter. Aristotle saw God as the first cause of an eternal universe. Ancient Near-Eastern mythologies saw creation as generated by gods through conflict or union. But the Bible stands in stark contrast to all of these. There was nothing, and then God created everything. He brought everything into being. He created the universe; he did not just craft it. This is the basis of God's power and authority over nature. He made it, he runs it, he owns it.

Not many people would dispute that this is what the Bible says. It is less well understood that God *runs* nature, that he keeps it going, moment by moment under his deliberate attention. Although this is one of the most basic ideas of the Bible, this truth is usually left out of a great deal of discussion about God and nature. It is a pity, for understanding God's continual supervision and upholding of creation is crucial to understanding what the Bible says about nature.

Why is this so poorly understood? Again, we might remember our Puritan William Perkins and his prophecy about the way humans are likely to understand the universe. We are all too ready to forget that the mechanism does not just run on its own. We get to be so entranced by the clock that we forget the clockmaker.

Of course, clockwork itself can be a rather misleading analogy. If we think of intricacies of the universe as being like a superbly crafted clock, then we can easily think of it as something that *does* run on its own. Such an understanding leads us to what is generally known as deism, the view that God is a distant creator who set the clock ticking and thereafter left it alone to run or break down as it will. It is not a biblical view, but it is easy enough for even Bible-believers to slip into. We see physical causes for events and think that is enough. We forget that God's continual power is behind every physical cause.

God as he is described in the Bible, however, never goes away to leave the world on its own. If he did, the world would simply cease to exist. There is no power in matter that is inherent within it. What makes the universe work is God's continued decision to keep it working. Every event happens because God makes it happen. He makes the grass grow. He provides food, water, and light. He determines the number of the stars. He controls weather systems and ecologies and populations. Creation is not something he merely made; it is something he makes happen.

If that is the case, then how is the Bible at all compatible with science? Surely science works on the premise that the universe is causal and regular? How can this fit with the idea that a god controls nature by fiat?

If we were talking about a fickle god, then that objection would be valid, but we are not. We are talking about the biblical God, who not only rules everything but does so in a regular, trustworthy way. This is a second fundamental concept that is crucial to understanding God and nature: God's character.

GOD IS NOT CAPRICIOUS

God delights in being trustworthy and dependable. His normal way of acting is through regular, patterned causes. He sets up systems of doing things, and he keeps to them. He keeps planets moving in their orbits. He keeps seasons coming, year after year. He keeps the cycles of life going.

This is the kind of predictability that science depends upon. In the normal functioning of the universe, systems keep on behaving in the same way under the same conditions. The way light travels in a vacuum on earth is the same way it travels in a vacuum in outer space. Oxygen molecules are the same in England as in Peru as in some distant galaxy. There is an orderliness and repeatability to reality that we can depend upon.

This is reflected in the way that science can use mathematical models to understand the world. Mathematics, that most abstract and logical of disciplines, is directly applicable to the real world because the real world behaves logically. Whether population genetics or the movement of planets, the predictable behavior of the world can be captured in mathematical equations. It's the reason that computer models can be built to simulate real-world systems. There is a basic orderliness to creation that can be expressed in simple principles that lie behind all the complexity of reality.

The logic of the world is no accident. Indeed, if it were an accident, it would be totally incredible. The world is orderly and logical because God is reasonable and trustworthy. He wants the world to run in a well-organized fashion, and he makes sure it does so. The orderly characteristics of the world are based in God's character, which is both rational and faithful. He does not act on whims. He is not capricious. He can be trusted to be consistent. He does what he says he will do, and his character does not change. He made a world to reflect the way that he is himself, and he keeps it running that way.

GOD'S REASON FOR CREATION

Certainly God could have made the world in any way that occurred to him. He chose to make it in an organized and rational way because, the Bible says, he had a particular purpose. It was not just for fun or to test out a few theories. It was not an exercise in experimental physics. It was something he created deliberately, and part of his purpose was to have humans living within the world he created.

The world was not created to remain empty. God wanted life, and he wanted human life. He made a habitable world, and part of that means consistency. The pattern of the world is one that makes human habitation possible. It is a world that supports life and particularly the learning that is necessary for humans to sustain their own lives. It is a world in which agriculture is possible because there are predictable seasons and ways of planting and growing. It is a world in which animals follow certain patterns, a world in which ecosystems can be understood; it is a world in which there are predictors of future events that can be studied and grasped.

God is rational, wise, and trustworthy, and he created a world that he wanted humans to be able to inhabit. We are capable of emulating God's wisdom, at least to some extent, the Bible says, because God has created the kind of world that we can learn from. We live in a world that makes sense. The world is not fundamentally chaotic. The physical world is not an illusion, as some philosophies would have it. It is not evil, as certain religious views might teach. God has created a world that is good, and he expects us to live in it and learn from it. We are expected to come to understand the way that cause and effect works in the world and draw general principles from that. It is not made purely for our intellectual satisfaction, but it is the kind of world that can be immensely intellectually satisfying because God designed it to make sense.

DOES THE BIBLE ENCOURAGE KNOWLEDGE?

It's a famous tactic of the "science against religion" lobby to assert that the Bible encourages people to be narrow-minded, against research, and against progress in knowledge. Fortunately for science, that has never been true.

We have seen that the Bible presents us with a view of the world that is organized and ready for us to inhabit. As part of that, we would expect to be able to understand how the world works. Not surprisingly, then, the Bible encourages people to go ahead and investigate the world in order to understand and take care of it. As we have seen, this is part of what comes under the category "wisdom": investigating the world and coming to understand it.

A lot of the knowledge thus gained is of practical use for everyday living. The Bible does not just talk about religious knowledge; it encourages the sort of observation and learning through experience that anyone with sense can gain and from which anyone would benefit. Indeed, some of it is directly parallel with quite non-religious writings from ancient Egypt.

Nor is the knowledge just for the sake of human advancement. King Solomon, renowned as the wisest of all Israelites, indeed internationally famous for his wisdom, undertook the study of the natural world as part of gaining of knowledge. He studied "trees, from the cedar that is in Lebanon to the hyssop that grows out of the wall. He spoke also of beasts, and of birds, and of reptiles, and of fish" (1 Kgs 4:33–34). This is a small point within a much wider story, but one worth noting.

A MARRED WORLD?

Of course, on another level it seems ridiculous to talk of the world as not being chaotic. For a lot of people, it seems very chaotic most of the time. Droughts come and destroy the harvest. Crops fail. Diseases turn up out of nowhere. The stronger the antibiotics get, the stronger the bugs get. Wars happen. Families fall apart. For most people chaos and suffering seem to be what life is about, at least some of the time.

That is true, and that is a different part of the story that is extremely important to the Bible and that naturalism does not explain. This world is fundamentally good, inhabitable, understandable, and rational. It has also been marred. "Cursed" is the way the Bible puts it (Gen 3:17), as a result of the wrong-headedness of people who refuse to acknowledge God as the creator and life-giver that he is. God could have, of course, destroyed the entire world at the first sign of rebellion. He's not that kind of God, so he didn't. Humanity's rebellion, nonetheless, had consequences for the natural world, and the harmony in which humans originally lived with the rest of creation was disrupted.

The refusal of humanity to acknowledge God as he deserves is the problem of sin, and its solution is what most of the Bible is concerned with. It is not what this book is meant to be about, so we will not be going further into the issue here. However, it is far more important than any philosophy, so do investigate further.[38]

That also brings us to our next point. There are limits to our knowledge. Some knowledge in particular lies beyond what we can work out for ourselves.

THE LIMITS OF NATURAL KNOWLEDGE

There are some things that we will never discover or be able to explain simply by studying the world. God created the universe for Christ, not for us, nor for our pleasure in investigation, nor for itself. God created us, humanity itself, for Christ, and he intends humanity to be like Christ. We will never understand what it is to be human and will never be fully human until we take seriously our purpose in being created for Christ.

This is where naturalism fails us entirely. Yes, one can live without belief in God and even enjoy the many good things of this world, including natural knowledge, for a time. But there will still be something absolutely crucial missing: what it is all for. Denying that there is any such thing is no answer. Naturalism, by its very nature, cannot tell us what life is about because life is about something beyond this universe. It is real, and it is essential. Without this crucial knowledge, we will never be truly human because that knowledge is central to why we were made.

Knowing that we and the world were made for Christ also makes sense of any other knowledge we have. It puts everything in context. It now makes sense that we are people who are capable of and seek knowledge. It is not a meaningless aberration of evolution. It is part of who God created us to be. That we have the ability to research, invent, and discover as well as the crippling tendency to destroy and argue makes sense when we see who we were meant to be and how we have fought against it. Knowing what we were made for is the only thing that can give meaning to all our other knowledge. It is the only thing that can actually turn knowledge into wisdom.

So what do we make of this? What does the Bible tell us about a realistic attitude toward the natural world and the ways in which we study it?

PUTTING IT ALL TOGETHER

Discovering how the natural world works is a God-given ability and a worthy task. We could not do it if God had not created the world as it is and us as we are. As God's creatures with the responsibility to live in God's world and look after it (although God entirely controls it), we are in a position to understand a great deal about it.

What we discover about the world—whatever true knowledge the scientific enterprise comes up with—cannot possibly do away with the need for God. There is no such thing as a natural cause that is an alternative to God as cause. God is behind every causal process. The Theory of Everything in its absolute, most complete form, even if absolutely and accurately true, would be only a complement to understanding God as cause. It could never give reason to say God does not exist. God is not in competition with his world. He makes it happen.

God was never an explanatory theory put there to make sense of a world that was otherwise inexplicable. The Bible never presents the complexity of the world as an argument for believing in God. It is entirely the other way around. The fact of the existence of the creator God is why people should accept the complexity of the world and tackle it with confidence, knowing that knowledge is possible. God as explanation can never be replaced by scientific explanation. He is the reason for scientific explanation.

Moreover, he is infinitely creative, so we can never sit back, content that we have understood everything. God's very creativity is a basis for the empirical method in investigation. We cannot second-guess God. We need to go out there and discover what he has done. This was very important in the early days of science. Part of the impetus to begin experimental science was the argument that we cannot deduce from first principles what God must do in the world. We can only go and discover what he has done. This is what makes science so exciting.[39]

Contrast this with what the alternative would be if there were no God. If we had no reason whatsoever to expect the world to be consistent and investigable, if we had no confidence that underneath the changeable surface there are deep regularities and patterns to reality, why would we persist with the hard work of science? What motivation could we have in the face of repeated failed experiments to press on to knowledge? It is only the reality of the creator God that makes science possible. Naturalism, the idea that science dismisses the need for God, is a weak, and very flawed, imitation.

It is to naturalism itself, and its poor record of explaining our universe, that we now turn. For indeed its record is poor on many levels.

5

THE PROBLEMS
OF NATURALISM

T HE BIBLE ESTABLISHES a strong case against naturalism: without God, we have no basis for understanding the world, neither for what is within the scope of science and certainly not for what lies outside it. On the other hand, accepting that the biblical God is real and active gives a thorough basis for confidence in looking at and understanding the natural world.

Finally, we now consider what happens if we do away with this. Just suppose the naturalists are right. What if the natural world is all that exists? What if we have no resources for explanation or understanding other than what we can observe around us? What then?

THE PROBLEM OF POWER

Theologian Colin Gunton writes:

Is the universe in some way divine, in the sense that it accounts of itself for the way that it is, or is it the creation of an agent who is other than it, and, specifically, personal? Once the Bible has made its impact on human thought it is a recurring and unavoidable question. That such a distinction between two ontologies is inevitable is shown in the writings of some modern popularizers of science. ... It is the biologists, although not only they, who are now carrying the burden of proclaiming science as an alternative to religion, taking up the tasks that once fell to the priests, at least as they sometimes see the matter. Yet as we read some of them it appears to be the case that when the being of the world is no longer attributed to the personal agency of God it is itself made the bearer of divine or creative powers. In other words, something like a pantheism is generated.[40]

Where does the generative power of the universe come from? Why is it here at all, and what keeps it going? We have two alternatives: either the power comes from within or outside the universe. For naturalists, this is reduced to one alternative: the power comes from within the universe itself. Most naturalists would balk at being called pantheists, but that is very close to what they are saying. Naturalists are committed to saying that the creative power of matter comes from matter itself.

However there is an essential problem in claiming this, for the scientific conclusion from study of the natural universe itself is that the universe had a beginning. It is not eternally self-generating. It started from nothing. What made it start?

The questions do not stop there. Even if we take the universe as it is right now, what keeps it going? This is generally not recognized as such a big question. The simple answer is energy or the second law of thermodynamics, the imperative of entropy to increase, the arrow of time that leads from one end of the universe to the other. The mechanism keeps itself running in all the ways that we can describe in such detail. Causality marches on. One thing causes another, which causes another, which causes another. The beginning may be something worth discussion, but now that the beginning has happened, the ongoing process is not contentious.

Yet is it so simple? As David Hume pointed out some centuries ago, we never actually observe causation. We observe one thing happening, then another. We observe the same pattern of events happening hundreds of times. We see billiard ball A hitting billiard ball B and transferring its momentum. But all we actually observe is one event, then the next event: ball A moving, ball B moving. We do not actually observe causation.

We live in a universe that keeps on working reliably and consistently over time. Why? What makes it keep going in this causal fashion? Naturalism can give no answer. It just does, and let's be grateful that it does because if it did not we would not be here to ask the question.[41] Naturalism cannot accept a creator God who keeps it going. It must be content without having an explanation.

This is something to take seriously about naturalism. The choice between Christianity and naturalism is not the choice between different types of explanation. It is the choice between having an explanation or not having one at all. Unlike God, the universe does not contain its explanation within it. The universe itself testifies to the fact that it had a beginning, and it is proceeding to an end. Why? Alone, the universe cannot tell us.

THE PROBLEM OF MORALITY

Every human society has had some system of morality, generally agreed and enforced rules about what is right and wrong, what humans ought to do in their conduct toward each other. Almost every human being, as far as we know, has an internalized set of rules about what he or she ought to do in certain situations. We usually call such sets of rules morals and the field that discusses and theorizes morality ethics.

Where do the rules about right and wrong come from?

We have a few choices. Perhaps it is something we have worked out as intelligent beings who need to get along somehow. We decide which rules work best and agree with each other to abide by them. Crudely speaking, this is the view known as utilitarianism.

We might also think that there are certain rules of good behavior that are innate to human nature. We are social animals. It is not surprising if built into our sociable nature is a certain understanding of how to get along. You may think this is a useful survival strategy and not at all surprising. Many evolutionists hold this view.[42]

A third view, and one that naturalism does not support, is that ethics come from God. God decides what is right and wrong, and only God can decide. This view is decidedly unpopular among many people these days. It is seen not just as outdated, but arrogant, intolerant, and denying human dignity.

Let us consider the alternatives.

The Christian view is that God is a personal creator and has made us as responsible creatures. We are responsible for ourselves, each other, and the world he gave us.

Naturalistic ethics will, in general, utterly deny this. In any purely evolutionary schema, we are just matter that merely evolved the way we evolved. Here we are, and we just are. Our ethics can consistently reflect only this. A purely naturalistic ethic recognizes that we are meaningless organisms, purposelessly evolved matter on one unimportant branch of the evolutionary tree. We are not beings created to love and care for each other with responsibilities, duties, and moral expectations. We are merely animals, and the fittest will survive.

This makes for an easy solution to many ethical problems. "I don't see what the fuss is," stated one politician about the issue of experimenting on human embryos. "I've looked down the microscope, and they're just a bunch of cells." That answer is entirely consistent with naturalism. Of course an embryo is just a bunch of cells. Why make a fuss over it? It does not matter. Experiment on it if you like.

The problem is that the politician himself is no different. He, too, is just a bunch of cells. A bigger bunch, granted, but what does that matter? If someone wants to experiment on him, why not?

If there is nothing but the natural world around us, then we don't matter. We can do whatever we like to each other because there is no sin. If there is no God, then there is no sin. We can answer the uncomfortable question of the judgment of God by dispensing with God. If we get rid of God and his relationship with man, then we get rid of the judgment of God.

The trouble is that if you are not created by God, if you are not held accountable by God, then you have no meaning or purpose. Not many people applaud this idea. Dispense with God and yes, you lose the problem of evil, but you also lose people. You lose humanity. There is nothing wrong, then, with eliminating people who have diseases. They are just animals that have gone wrong, and we know what to do with diseased animals: we cull them.

It is not only humanity that fails to matter if there is nothing more than the natural world. Ironically, the natural world ceases to matter as well. It is just a collection of atoms. Some of us like our collections of atoms in the form of trees and meadows. Others prefer cars and fuel. Who is to say which is better? There is no value to be attached to the world other than what any individual cares to give it; and no individual matters more than another. It just comes down to who has the power to make their values win.

But people do matter because they are made in the image of God. We should feel heartache over suffering. People do have dignity; they do have freedom and responsibility. We are responsible to care for each other. There are very few practical atheists in this world, thank God, for when most atheists face suffering, they still think it matters. They do not have any good reason to—but they do. It is when we see the truly hardened atheists that we see the real inhumanity and horror of such a view. Stalin was a truly consistent atheist. He did not think human suffering mattered. He made that quite clear.

Moreover, the natural world does matter because God made and values it. God gives a value to nature that humans cannot. He is the one who says it is important and that we have a responsibility to care for it because it is his. Naturalism cannot manage to protect the one thing it has: nature. Only God can give nature its true value.

If there is no God, we need not worry, for there will be no consequences. But if there is no God, then nothing matters, for there are no consequences. Which would you really prefer?

EXPLAINING HUMANS

There is more to explaining humans than simply explaining human ethics. That is certainly a major and intractable problem if you insist there is nothing other than the natural world. Humans are more complicated than that. If we are to account for reality, we need to account for the bizarre, contradictory, wonderful things that are human beings.

Humans are animals. We have physiology, anatomy, chemical structure, and a whole host of other describable properties that are analogous with other animals. We exist as physical matter. We eat, survive, and reproduce. Physically, we are objects for scientific study in the same way that any other organism can be. From the minute level of biochemistry up to the level of observable behavior and anthropology, we can be understood as animals and as part of the interwoven network of organisms that make up the biological world.

Why, then, are we so outlandishly different from other animals?

It is truly astonishing that this question is so easily brushed aside. Television documentaries, science journalism, and school textbooks make the most of the similarity between humans and other animals. We are told of our anatomical structures that are analogous with birds, reptiles, and other mammals and the ways in which human embryology goes through similar developmental stages. We are educated that chimpanzees can display complex social behavior and that other anthropoids can use tools or hunt intelligently. These are emphasized most when we examine the natural world. Of course, it makes sense that we would look for similarities. If nothing else, we are self-absorbed creatures, and what interests us most about other animals is the way in which we can identify with them. Makers of television documentaries understand this and so cater to their audience.

We are so used to looking at the similarities between ourselves and other creatures, however, that we can miss the truly amazing fact that for all our similarities—for all our common DNA and shared traits and anatomy—humans stand out as the only species that actually rules the world. Certainly we rule it badly. We are destructive, selfish, and wantonly cruel. But even the failures of our rule still make us stand out against the rest of the animal world. We are, simply, very different.

How are we to account for this? In physical terms, it does not make much sense. We share so much in common, physically, with other animals. We have, it appears, 97 percent of the same DNA as chimpanzees. The actual genetic difference is tiny, yet we are not chimpanzees or really anything like them. Why is it that a 97 percent chimpanzee manages to conquer the highest mountains and the depth of the seas, dominate any habitat, survive in the most wide-ranging and hostile of environments, discover the fundamental particles of matter itself, go into space, overcome disease, and even investigate the very nature of life, when a 100 percent chimpanzee does not? Why are we concerned with justice, love, linguistics, communication, and society? What could make a 97 percent chimpanzee being like this? The 97 percent similarity does not prove that we are "just" apes. It proves that there is something very strange about being human.

It is not at all surprising that Darwin's theory of human descent from apes created such outrage when it was first suggested, and this outrage cannot be attributed solely to religious arrogance. If it is true that humans evolved from ape-like ancestors with a pedigree not different in kind from any other anthropoid, then there is a huge amount that needs explaining. These days we are so familiar with the theory that we forget how much it fails to explain humanity. At least when people believed in the special creation of humans, there was a satisfying explanation for why humans are so different from other animals. If we are to believe instead in evolutionary descent, or any other entirely naturalistic theory, we need much more.

A naturalistic theory of humanity—whether it is Darwinian evolution or any other theory that might come along—still has a lot of explaining to do. It is not good enough to reduce our conception of humanity to fit the convenience of a naturalistic theory. Any theory has to cope with reality. We are not, actually, just intelligent apes. We are beings with extraordinary abilities to conquer, dominate, and change our world. We are beings with concepts of meaning, responsibility, and love.

There is a common naturalistic story told about the progress of human ideas. Once upon a time, the story goes, we used to believe that we lived in the center of the universe and were the most important part of God's creation. We were arrogant and ignorant, and religion conspired to keep us that way. Gradually, however, the forces of humanity and reason began to exert themselves. Heroes arose from time to time with new ideas that brought us closer to truth. And although religion usually killed these heroes and tried to suppress their ideas, reason and the human spirit could not be suppressed forever, and so slowly we began to progress away from our superstitious, dark roots.

One of these heroes, the story goes, was Copernicus, who discovered that the earth is not at the center of the universe, but instead revolves around the sun. He, like his follower Galileo, was cowed and beaten by religious authority, but the idea still spread, and so humanity was dethroned from its place at the center of the universe. Later on, another hero, Darwin, told us that we were not the peak of God's creation, but in fact descended from other animals, and so we humbly accepted our place alongside them. Human reason told us the truth: we are not so special or different after all.

Historically, the story is largely nonsense, but that is for another discussion.[43] The point to be made here is, even if it were true, humans have done a very bad job at becoming humble. We will not be dethroned. For all our faults, we keep hitting up against the inconvenient reality (for this picture) that we are, in fact, more than animals. The real problem is how to account for the undeniable difference that exists.

Yet how are we to do this without God? If all we have is the natural world, then all we can appeal to are natural characteristics. We can talk about evolved intelligence, even though that does not really account for the moral realities that we observe in human responsibility for the planet. We can talk about the acquisition of language and social structures and even an evolved need for a religious sense. We can transfer religious awe to nature and talk about evolution in a semi-mystical way. It is very common for naturalistic apologists to fill science with religious imagery in an attempt to satisfy religious feeling with awe of science, evolution, or human history.[44]

Naturalism alone does not account for the complex reality that humanity is. In our very attempts to theorize and understand ourselves as an equal part of nature, we demonstrate our inequality. Naturalism fails to explain humanity. It can deny or reduce it, but it does not explain it.

6

CONCLUSION

I T HAS TAKEN a long time for our society to reach a point where naturalism is easily accepted. It has been a difficult fight on the part of determined naturalists to get us here. We are currently bombarded with the views of fervent atheists who still feel the need to keep us from questioning this particular worldview.

In many ways naturalism is an easy philosophy to slip into. It does not demand much of us. It leaves us without any particular responsibility. It can even feel intellectually humble by not postulating entities unnecessarily. It can feel as if one is, simply, not going beyond the evidence.

The easiness of the philosophy is deceptive. Accept naturalism, and you enter a bewildering universe in which there is no necessary reason to accept that things will continue on as they always have, that they will be understandable, or that anything will make sense at all. It is a universe in which you are merely another bit of stray matter fighting for survival among all the other bits of stray matter. It is a universe in which your consciousness is an unfortunate side-effect of complexity. It is unfortunate because it enables you to ask questions that will never be answered and enables you to be aware of the agony of existence that does not mean anything.

It is also an entirely unnecessary philosophy. There is no need at all for the contortions that well-meaning materialists go to in order to understand the universe, humanity, the existence of life, or the eternal struggle for harmony. The tools are all there and all perfectly accessible for those who would actually like to know the truth.

This has been a short excursion into naturalism and the Bible's response to it, and no doubt there is much more you would like to have explained. Below are a few books that will provide a start. Make the effort. The understanding is well worth it.

Acknowledgments

THE SERIES Questions for Restless Minds is produced by the Christ on Campus Initiative, under the stewardship of the editorial board of D. A. Carson (senior editor), Douglas Sweeney, Graham Cole, Dana Harris, Thomas McCall, Geoffrey Fulkerson, and Scott Manetsch. The editorial board recognizes with gratitude the many outstanding evangelical authors who have contributed to this series, as well as the sponsorship of Trinity Evangelical Divinity School (Deerfield, Illinois), and the financial support of the MAC Foundation and the Carl F. H. Henry Center for Theological Understanding. The editors also wish to thank Christopher Gow, who created the study questions accompanying each book, and Todd Hains, our editor at Lexham Press. May God alone receive the glory for this endeavor!

Study Guide Questions

1. How did Francis Bacon describe the relationship between God and natural philosophy?

2. Why was Paley's watch story ultimately misleading in its message about the relationship between God and science?

3. In what sense are some definitions of science tautologous (see page 29)?

4. Birkett claims that "science is possible only because of God" (51). What do you make of this claim? How does she defend it?

5. How do Christian convictions motivate scientific inquiry?

6. Birkett cites the problems of power, morality, and humans as areas where naturalism fails to deliver acceptable answers. What are these problems, and which do you find most

problematic for naturalism as a theory? What answers does Christianity provide to these problems?

7. What do you find encouraging about Christianity's answers to these big questions?

8. Spend some time this week contemplating God's relationship to/with creation; thank God for his providential care and reliable character that make life possible.

For Further Reading

These works are recommended introductions to the vast literature on the interaction between science and Christianity:

Alexander, Denis. *Rebuilding the Matrix: Science and Faith in the 21st Century*. Lion, 2001.

Birkett, Kirsten Renée. *Unnatural Enemies: An Introduction to Science and Christianity*. Matthias Media, 1997.

Desmond, Adrian. *Huxley: From Devil's Disciple to Evolution's High Priest*. Penguin, 1997.

Forster, Roger and V. Paul Marston. *Reason, Science and Faith*. Monarch, 1999.

Pearcey, Nancy R., and Charles B. Thaxton. *The Soul of Science: Christian Faith and Natural Philosophy*. Crossway, 1994.

Russell, Colin Archibald. *Cross-Currents: Interactions Between Science and Faith*. Eerdmans, 1985.

Notes

1. Francis Crick, *The Astonishing Hypothesis: The Scientific Search for the Soul* (Touchstone, 1995), 3, 6.
2. Richard Dawkins, *The God Delusion* (Black Swan, 2007), 57.
3. Bertrand Russell, *Religion and Science* (Oxford University Press, 1935), 243.
4. Edward O. Wilson, *The Creation: An Appeal to Save Life on Earth* (Norton, 2006), 3–4.
5. See Stewart Goetz and Charles Taliaferro, *Naturalism* (Eerdmans, 2008), for a discussion of different kinds of naturalism.
6. Richard Dawkins is probably the most famous British advocate of atheism. The expatriate British journalisst Christopher Hitchens has written widely in the United States. In Australia, Phillip Adams advocates similar views.
7. This is despite many practicing scientists being theists, including Francis Collins (director of the National Human Genome Research Institute) and computational and theoretical chemist Fritz

Schaeffer. There are thousands of other examples. See, for example, R. J. Berry, ed., *Real Science, Real Faith* (Monarch, 1991).

8. There is also what is known as "methodological naturalism." This is a mode of doing, say, scientific experiments, assuming that whatever natural phenomenon is being studied will have a natural explanation. It leaves unasked and unanswered questions about ultimate explanations and is frequently the heuristic used by theistic scientists in their day-to-day scientific work. It is in many ways a misleading term, as the scientist may believe firmly that God is entirely responsible for the natural activity being studied, but the scientist is just not interested in that question at the moment. As we will see, there are various historical reasons for why many Christians take this approach to the natural world, assuming that natural events have natural causes, even if ultimately the overall cause is God. It is a very different position from what we are calling naturalism in this book (the metaphysical position that the natural world, as opposed to any supernatural world, is the only thing that exists).

9. There are many different ways of categorizing causation; we are looking at one simple schema here. Another important part of the Scientific Revolution was the way in which Aristotle's "final

cause" was excluded from the workings of science; this was also discussed in Bacon's work.

10. Francis Bacon, *The Advancement of Learning and New Atlantis* (Oxford University Press, 1960), 11.

11. Thomas Sprat, *History of the Royal Society* (1667), 63.

12. Sprat, *History of the Royal Society*, 82.

13. See the discussion in Stephen Shapin, *The Scientific Revolution* (University of Chicago Press, 1996), 135–55.

14. William Perkins, *Foure great lyers, striuig who shall win the siluer Whetstone. Also, a resolvtion to the countri-man, prouing it vtterly unlawfull to buye or use our yeerly prognostications*, 1608, W. 1585; STC 19080, spelling updated.

15. William Paley, *Natural Theology,* in the *Miscellaneous Works of William Paley* 3 (Baldwyn, 1821), 9–11.

16. This is not a fair summary of the whole of Paley's writings. We are concerned here with the ideas that influence popular perceptions about God and science.

17. Charles Darwin, "Autobiography," in Francis Darwin, *The Life of Charles Darwin* (John Murray, 1902; reprint, Studio Editions, 1995), 18.

18. This is exactly how Richard Dawkins responds to Paley's argument: "Paley's argument is made with

passionate sincerity and is informed by the best biological scholarship of his day, but it is wrong, gloriously and utterly wrong. All appearances to the contrary, the only watchmaker in nature is the blind forces of physics, albeit deployed in a very special way." Without Darwin's explanation of apparent design, Dawkins says, it would have been very difficult to resist Paley's argument, but "Darwin made it possible to be an intellectually fulfilled atheist" (Richard Dawkins, *The Blind Watchmaker* [Penguin, 1988], 5–6).

19. See how Richard Dawkins presents the argument from design: "Things in the world, especially living things, look as though they have been designed. Nothing that we know looks designed unless it is designed. Therefore there must have been a designer, and we call him God. ... The argument from design is the only one still in regular use today, and it still sounds to many like the ultimate knockdown argument. ... Unfortunately for Paley, the mature Darwin blew it out of the water" (Richard Dawkins, *The God Delusion* [Black Swan, 2007], 103).

20. Charles Darwin, *The Origin of Species by Means of Natural Selection, or The Preservation of Favored Races in the Struggle for Life* (Penguin, 1968), 169–70.

21. Francis Darwin, *The Life of Charles Darwin*, 58.

22. On Thomas Huxley, see Adrian Desmond's excellent work, *Huxley: From Devil's Disciple to Evolution's High Priest* (Penguin, 1997).

23. See Morris Berman, "'Hegemony' and the Amateur Tradition in British Science," *Journal of Social History* 8 (1975): 30–43.

24. Cyril Bibby, ed., *The Essence of T. H. Huxley: Selections from His Writings* (St. Martin's Press, 1967), 8.

25. For a description of this campaign, see J. V. Jensen, "The X Club: Fraternity of Victorian Scientists," *The British Journal for the History of Science* 5 (1970): 63–72; R. M. MacLeod, "The X-club: A Scientific Network in Late Victorian England," *Notes and Records of the Royal Society* 24 (1970): 305–322; Edward Caudill, "The Bishop-Eaters: The Publicity Campaign for Darwin and *On the Origin of Species*," *Journal of the History of Ideas* 55 (1994): 441–66; and David Starling, "Thomas Huxley and the 'Warfare' Between Science and Religion: Mythology, Politics and Ideology," *kategoria* 3 (1996): 33–50.

26. Huxley, *Collected Essays* (New York: Greenwood, 1893), 1:41, quoted in F. M. Turner, *Between Science and Religion: The Reaction to Victorian Scientific Naturalism in Late Victorian England* (Yale University Press, 1974), 17–18.

27. In Bibby, *Essence of T. H. Huxley*, 15. For further discussion of Huxley's campaign and his appropri-

ation of religious trappings, see Colin A. Russell, "The Conflict Metaphor and Its Social Origins," *Science and Christian Belief* 1 (1989): 3–26.

28. Huxley, "The Origin of Species" (1860), in *Collected Essays*, 2.52. This has been a tactic frequently used by anti-Christian polemicists. See J. W. Draper, *History of the Conflict Between Religion and Science* (Kegan Paul, Trench and Co., 1883) and A. D. White's *History of the Warfare of Science with Theology in Christendom* (Appleton, 1898).

29. See note 14.

30. Parts of this section are taken from my essay, "What Is Science?" published in *kategoria* 7 (1997): 29–50.

31. Lee Smolin, *The Life of the Cosmos* (Weidenfeld and Nicolson, 1997).

32. For a classic discussion of what a scientific "law" is, see Ernest Nagel, *The Structure of Science: Problems in the Logic of Scientific Explanation* (Routledge and Kegan Paul, 1961).

33. A useful text on historical justifications of scientific method is David Oldroyd, *The Arch of Knowledge: An Introductory Study of the History of the Philosophy and Methodology of Science* (New South Wales University Press, 1986).

34. See Karl R. Popper, *Conjectures and Refutations: The Growth of Scientific Knowledge* (Routledge and Kegan Paul, 1963) and *The Logic of Scientific Discovery* (Hutchinson, 1980).

35.   See for instance Peter Lipton, "Is the Best Good
      Enough?" in David Papineau, ed., *The Philosophy of
      Science* (Oxford University Press, 1996), 93–106.

36.   See Larry Laudan, "A Confutation of Convergent
      Realism," in *The Philosophy of Science*, 107–38.

37.   This trend was famously introduced by the
      physicist Thomas Kuhn in *The Structure of Sci-
      entific Revolutions* (University of Chicago Press,
      1962). A further revision of his ideas can be found
      in "Second Thoughts on Paradigms," in Freder-
      ick Suppe, ed., *The Structure of Scientific Theories*
      (University of Illinois Press, 1977), 459–82. For a
      critique see Frederick Suppe, "Exemplars, Theo-
      ries and Disciplinary Matrixes," in *The Structure
      of Scientific Theories* (483–99). See also Suppe's
      "Introduction" and "Afterword" in the same volume
      (3–232, 617–730).

38.   See Graham A. Cole, *What Is a Christian World-
      view?* (Lexham Press, 2022).

39.   See the discussion in John Hedley Brooke, *Science
      and Religion: Some Historical Perspectives* (Cam-
      bridge University Press, 1991).

40.   Colin E. Gunton, *The Triune Creator: A Historical
      and Systematic Study* (Eerdmans, 1998), 37.

41.   This is a reply that often turns up in discussion
      of the anthropic principle. See Denis Alexander,
      *Rebuilding the Matrix: Science and Faith in the 21st
      Century* (Lion, 2001).

42. For more on this, see Alexander, *Rebuilding the Matrix*.

43. See Philip Sampson's *Six Modern Myths* (IVP, 2000).

44. Richard Dawkins is a prime example of this tendency. See also Edward O. Wilson.